Jarrow
in old picture postcards

by Paul Perry

European Library ZALTBOMMEL/THE NETHERLANDS

About the author:

Paul Perry was born and raised in Jarrow, where he pursued a career in photography. After learning his profession, he operated a studio in the town, and it was from here, Paul was introduced to the delights of local history. In 1966 he became involved with collecting old photographs of his home town, his fascination, and collection swelled beyond all expectations. To date, Paul has amassed many thousands of photographs of Jarrow, and neighbouring Hebburn, and is no stranger to the written word. In 1991 and in 1992, he was responsible for writing the popular 'Portrait of old Jarrow' volumes 1 and 2. In 1996 he was co-author of 'Curiosities of County Durham', and has recently completed a quiz book on the County.

Acknowledgements:

I am most grateful to the following people, and organizations for their co-operation: Frank and Kathleen Weir, Lord and Lady Dixon, Margaret Connacher, Kelly, Angela, and Anthony Perry, staff of the local history departments of Newcastle and South Tyneside Libraries, and the people of Jarrow, for their continued support and encouragement.

GB ISBN 90 288 1120 6

© 1998 European Library – Zaltbommel/The Netherlands

Introduction

Should the Vikings ever return to Jarrow – or Gyrwy as it was called at the time of their last notorious visit in the year AD 866 – the blue-eyed, blonde, Scandinavian warriors would surely be presented with a different place to plunder. The six hundred monks which inhabited the monastery, on the banks of the Tyne where they moored their fleet of longboats, are no longer a feature of our town.

It is in fact many centuries since the eerie echo of a monk's chant was heard in the crumbling cloisters at Donmouth, as Gyrwy was often referred to. Bede, a mere child at the tender age of twelve years, was adopted by the brethren, and was to spend his whole life within the security of the monastery walls. He was to grow up a man of great learning mastering everything before him, Bede became re-known throughout the literary world with his 'Northumbrian Chronicles' and the numerous works the magical monk left us.

Donmouth at this time consisted of not many more than nine or ten cottages and a few hides of farmland, centered around the little church and monastery, which we know today as 'Low Jarrow'. It was about this time the area was to establish the basis of a hamlet, hence the commencement of our town. The significance of coal mining in Jarrow began modestly in 1803. With the inauguration of the Alfred Pit by Simon Temple, son of a wealthy South Shields shipbuilder. A shaft, 840 feet deep, was sunk to recover coal from a seam a mere six feet thick. As further coal seams were discovered, more labour was required to surface the precious black fuel. White-walled cottages were built by the caring Temple to house his growing army of workers. Seventeen-hour shifts at the coal face became necessary for the success of the town's first major industry.

As entrepreneur Temple persued other interests, he assigned importer and shipowner William Brown to manage the colliery in his absence. It is believed, through mis-management and a bankruptcy order looming in 1806, Temple was forced to make radical decisions by putting the colliery he had worked so hard for, into the care of the leaseholders of the St. Hilda & Harton Collieries at South Shields.

Because of substandard ventilation systems, and inadequate safety regulations, tragedy, inevitably, was never far away, many hundreds of men and boys lost their lives at the colliery prior to its closure in 1851. Simon Temple died a broken man in 1822 aged 63, bankrupt, penniless and homeless, at the home of one of his former manservants. A tragic end to a fine industrialist. Over the centuries, Jarrow has been host to many industries, from sail making to the production of stained glass, doubtless many of them were what we would term today as 'cottage industry'.

But what certainly could not qualify for that particular termin-

ology was the Palmer Shipbuilding Empire. Charles Mark
Palmer was born on 11th May 1822, son of shipping merchant
George and his wife Maria. In 1851 together with his brother
George, they set up the business of Palmer Bros & Co. Their first
vessel was a simple tug boat, but things were to take on a different dimention, gathering speed the company was to become
the most prolific shipbuilder in the country employing 10,000
men, women and boys, to build its quality craft for the Admir-
alty and indeed the world market. It was oft times said, and
even quoted: 'Palmers build ships by the yard, and sever them at
the required length.' One thousand ships sailed from Palmers
docks, before its doors finally closed in 1933.

1 This was, and still is today, the busiest junction in Jarrow. There has always been activity of one kind or another at this meeting place. Just about every one of the buildings in Jarrow were blackened with sooty deposits, a direct result of the heavy industry Jarrow enjoyed during a boom time. This photograph from 1932 shows unemployed men idling time away on street corners, evidence of the collapsing Palmer empire. No one realised it at the time, but things were to get worse, much worse. The halcyon days were rapidly diminishing as the depression tightened its powerful grip. The Mechanics Institute visible here to the right of the photograph was a gift to the town courtesy of Charles Mark Palmer, and used for reading rooms and social gatherings.

Ben Lomond Hotel, Jarrow 12677

2 Opened in 1902, the town hall is located in the centre of this busy little picture from 1908. Notice the absence of the clock, which wasn't erected until 1951 at a cost of £1,000. The Station Hotel is to the right of the photograph. It seems like the Ben Lomond hotel has squatted midway up Grange Road since the beginning of time, in actual fact, it was built towards the end of the 19th century. In 1970 it was refurbished and renamed the Viking. The tiny South Shields Gas Co was eventually swallowed up by the Northern Gas Board, who incidentally were relocated on the site left by the Station Hotel after it was demolished to make way for the shopping centre.

GRANGE ROAD, JARROW. 554.

3   Ninety Two Ormonde Street was the address of chemist William Penman, this can be verified by Wards directory, who produced a chronicle of businesses in towns and villages nationwide, and updated annually. Penman was not only an acknowledged chemist, he was also a highly thought of town councillor, who served the electorate in the Jarrow ward. The first sitting of the newly-formed council was in 1875. It was deemed right, and fitting the prominent position of councillor, was entrusted to the town's leading citizens, many of them being local businessmen. The advertisement for the 'Jarrow Express' in this quaint little photograph from 1912 doesn't bear any resemblance to a railway, or have anything to do with the tramcar ambling this way. It was, in fact, referring to the town's very own broadsheet newspaper established in 1868 and which, it is thought, survived until 1929.

Ormonde Street, Jarrow on Tyne

4   These three grocer boys in their crisp white starched aprons, proudly pose for the camera in the doorway of the London & Newcastle Tea Co in 1915. Practically every major town in the country had a branch of the 'L & N'. Jarrow must have been in a privileged position for it had two branches, the one pictured here in Ormonde Street, and another at Bede Burn Road – quality and freshness was their boast. Among the grocer boys' duties, along with serving behind the counter, were deliveries via hand cart. When Ormond Street was demolished in the 1960s, the 'L & N' like most other retail outlets in this once busy thoroughfare, had already moved into smart new premises in the shopping precinct. The Bede Burn Road branch closed in the early 1960s as part of the company's reorganisation programme, just prior to it being absorbed into the Lipton group of companies.

5   The Co-operative Society in this vicinity commenced as the Jarrow Industrial Co-operative in 1861, it wasn't until much later when it adopted the title of Jarrow & Hebburn Co-operative Society. The movement was to grow at an alarming rate, with scores of branches opening throughout the region. It rapidly became large enough to warrant the construction of swanky new offices in Albert Road in 1923. The public responded to the attractive dividend bonus scheme it offered, and shopping at the 'store' swiftly became a way of life. The Co-op charabanc is heavily laden with store managers, as it sets off for a day at the races.

6   Acres of land were donated to the townsfolk for recreation. The first being West Park, donated by wealthy Sir Walter and Lady James in 1876. In 1895, the stubborn Drewitt Ormonde Drewitt, inhabitant of Jarrow Hall, rejected the council's application for a donation of a piece of land to create a public park. After years of wrangling, he offered the land to the council at a nominal rent, who refused his miserly offer. It wasn't until Drewitt's death in 1910, that a field in front of Jarrow Hall was donated to the council by Alfred Chaytor, the adopted son of Drewitt. Eventually, the authorities announced the opening of the Drewitt playing fields in 1912, after seventeen argumentative years.

DREWETT PLAYING FIELDS, JARROW 2503

7   Green belted areas solely for the purpose of recreation were created just out of town at Primrose. A temperance ground became known as Springwell park, rose beds were developed along with sunken flower gardens and in 1921, the Longmore fountain, which stood for many years in the town centre, was relocated to a prime site in the park. Between Jarrow's four public parks, Springwell was the only one without amenities, it was, however, just a nice peaceful place to be. Paddling pools, tennis courts and bowling greens were among the attractions of the other parklands. This photograph of the tennis courts at Jarvis park dates from 1949.

8   Jarvis park lies juxtaposition with Springwell park, it serves as a memorial to Sir John Jarvis. Sir John came to Jarrow during those bleak desperate days of the 1930s, bringing with him the Surrey Fund. This money was donated by the people of affluent Surrey, to help feed and clothe the people of Jarrow during those terrible years of the depression. Sir John was instrumental in the setting up of the Jarrow Instruction Centre (J.I.C.), a centre teaching unemployed men, women, and boys new crafts. This photograph of Sir John touring the workshops was taken in 1934.

9   Unemployment was at its height in Jarrow in 1935 with 80 percent of the male working population out of work. The recent closure of the Palmer shipyard was to have a knock on effect with most other businesses – admittedly, none with the might, and power of Palmers – but nevertheless it was still a very bitter pill for the town to swallow. The situation was to become progressively worse, so bad in fact, in 1936 labour party stalwart Ellen Wilkinson M.P. chose 200 of the town's fittest men, with a hunger for work, to march 250 miles to London with a petition of 10,000 signatures in an attempt to inform Stanley Baldwin and his government, of the plight of our town. Somewhat disillusioned, the men returned to Jarrow, to the street corners, and few prospects. The government's abrupt refusal of assistance was a further blow to these proud men, who were simply fighting for the right to feed their families.

10 During the recovery years of the 1950s, as part of the authority's rehousing scheme, the residents in the central area of the town, were to be rehoused in modern new dwellings at the South Leam estate, in order to make way for a much needed bus station. A similar complex was under construction and nearing completion at Calf Close, a further site behind the cemetery was under consideration as another possibility, which eventually became Hill Park estate. The development of these satellite estates were designed to ease the population of what was rapidly becoming an overcrowded town. This unusual view of Grange Road as seen from the roof of the town hall comes from 1952. The Alnwick Castle hotel is in the immediate foreground, and opposite is the Salvation Army citadel.

11 Second time around, a trip to the 'flicks' has become fashionable, though not regarded today as the treat it once was yesteryear. There were five cinemas in Jarrow and Hebburn, evidence of which is displayed on this gable end. Whilst the three 'flea pits' in the town, the Empire, Picture House, and the Kino – latterly the Regal –, flourished, it was the Theatre Royal at Hebburn which was devastated by fire in 1949, and it was this atrocity which prompted the building of the Rex in Victoria Road. It is worthy of note, the premiere screening at the Rex was the Rock Hudson classic 'Magnificent Obsession'. This photograph of this well-appointed terrace in Ellison Street dates from the 1920s.

12 Above all else the one thing Jarrovians did extremely well was to build ships. Prior to his death in 1907, Charles Mark Palmer moulded his men, and taught them all there was to know about the shipbuilding industry, furnishing them with a comprehensive knowledge of every craft on the waterways of the world. Their expertise was reflected in the many hundreds of ships which sailed from the Tyne, with the guarantee 'no finer vessels were available anywhere'. The monster cantilevered, overhead cranes were built in Germany to Palmer's own specifications, and were to tower over the rooftops of Jarrow and indeed the whole of Tyneside for decades. The yard in 1927 was in full production with a 10,000 workforce and a healthy order book. Little did anyone realise then, but this world-famous shipyard was to grind to a standstill within a few short years. The ship in this photograph was named in her honour, and launched by her, H.R.H Duchess of York, in July 1928.

13 In 1902 sculptor Albert Toft was commissioned to fashion a statue of Sir Charles Mark Palmer, at a cost of 2,000, borne by his faithful workforce. In 1904, after a colourful ceremony witnessed by a large crowd of well-wishers, the statue was unveiled in the grounds of the hospital which Sir Charles built and dedicated to the memory of his first wife, where it was to remain for eighty years. After the completion of a landscaping programme on the south bank of the Tyne, it was thought befitting to relocate the statue close to the original site of his famous works. This photograph was taken in 1905.

14 This crudely built little wooden chair has stood somewhat awkward within the walls of St. Paul's Church for centuries. For many years it was believed the chair possessed magical powers: anyone sitting on it would be miraculously cured of any illness they may have. It was also a strong belief the chair was a cure for infertility, providing the infertile person removed a splinter of wood from it, evidence of which is in the accompanying photograph. Bede's chair, as it has always been known by, is nothing more than a tale, passed down for generations. Bede's bottom never actually graced the ancient little relic, as carbon dating revealed it was made in the eleventh century.

15   In the year A.D. 685, at the time of the dedication of St. Paul's Church at Donmouth, Benedict Biscop, a Northumbrian of considerable status, at the age of 25 abandoned excellent prospects to follow the ways of the Lord, in the hope of attaining the eternal Kingdom of Heaven. Several times Biscop travelled the long, and often perilous, journey to Rome. On the first occasion, it is believed, to be confirmed, and on each of the subsequent visits, he returned with books, and art treasures. It was on the return of his third visit to Rome, King Egfrid – son and heir to the late King Oswy – was greatly impressed with the actions of the gallant Biscop, at which he bestowed upon him a measure of land on the north side of the mouth of the River Wear for the purpose of building a monastery, this was to give its name to Monkwearmouth. King Egfrid was also suitably impressed with the monastery, he promptly granted Biscop forty hides (a hide being an ancient measure of land) at Donmouth on the Tyne estuary, and it was at this location he founded the monastery at Jarrow. This etching of the monastery ruins dates from around the 11th century.

16   Biscop chose twenty or so brothers from Monkwearmouth to form the new community on the banks of the River Don, and it was Ceolfrid, Biscop appointed to govern the new monastery. As the arduous task of the building work progressed, Biscop journeyed to Rome for the fifth time, this time returning with sacred pictures and artefacts for the monastery's embelishment. Eight years later in A.D. 673 Benedict Biscop was in ailing health, stricken with paralysis. His friend confidante and Abbot at Monkwearmouth Sigfrid, himself suffering from consumption, was beckoned to Donmouth to ease the suffering of the dying Biscop. Sigfrid never returned to Monkwearmouth, a short time after the death of Benedict Biscop, he too was called by the Lord.

17 Any publication about Jarrow would be incomplete without giving reference to the Venerable Bede. Much has been written about the great man, and it is a difficult task to write a concise passage about the 'Father of English Learning', when one considers the range of subjects to which he was familiar. In his cell, within the cloisters of the Jarrow monastery, the lamp of knowledge burned bright at his arrival, as a young boy of twelve, and it wasn't extinguished until after his death, half a century later. The many works Bede left us covered every aspect, of every subject known to man. This bilingual genius possessed an intensive knowledge of Hebrew, Greek, Latin and was fluent in the English tongue, which was at this time, very much in its infancy. Bede's final work was the translation into English, the Gospel of St. John, which was undertaken amidst ailing health, and a tremendous amount of painful suffering from chronic asthma. Bede passed away on 26th May 735, and was buried in a porch, in St. Paul's Church next to the monastery, where he rested for close to 300 years. Since 1020, Bede's re- mains have been encased in a tomb in Durham cathedral, a tomb befitting a man who gained respect from every scholar in the civilised world.

18 The handsome Victorian terraces to the right of this picture of Croft Terrace look as good today as they did when they were built more than one hundred years ago. Sadly the houses to the left survived only until the 1960s, demolished to make way for more modern dwellings. Croft Terrace mixed board school was completed ahead of schedule, and opened its doors in April 1894. The first intake of 550 children was very soon to experience a drastic shortage of staff, with in excess of 60 children crammed into every class-room, and one, with an amazing 89. The school is just visible at the top of this photograph from 1900.

Croft Terrace, Jarrow

19 Since early times, crossing the river to any point on the north side was somewhat of an ordeal. Since the beginning of the 20th century, both Jarrow and South Shields had a reliable ferry service to Howdon and North Shields respectively. The ferries were used by all modes of transport with the exception of a rail link. Although South Shields still operate a passenger ferry service, Jarrow has had a pedestrian tunnel for nearly fifty years. Work commenced in June 1947, and the 750,000 complex 90 feet under the bed of the river was ready for use in 1951. The tunnels, each 300 yards in length, and the escalators approaching them were 186 feet long – the worlds longest at this time.

Length of Tunnel - 300 yds. Length of Escalator - 186 ft.
Built in 1947 - Completed 1951.
Tunnel 90 ft under High Water Mark.   Cost - ¾ million.
JRW 19   Tyne Tunnel, Jarrow

20 Monkton village is situated straddling the border between Jarrow and Hebburn, it is reputed to be the birthplace of Bede, and it was from here he was taken to the Abbey of St. Peter at Monkwearmouth prior to going to the monastery at Jarrow. Whilst Monkton in its own right is an ancient place, the longest surviving property dates from the 14th or 15th century and with the exception of St. Paul's Church and monastery, boasts the oldest building in Jarrow. This view looking towards Hebburn, with the Lord Nelson inn to the right of the photograph, dates from 1898.

MONKTON VILLAGE NR JARROW

21 Monkton Leek, Vegetable and Floral Society was founded in 1864. Although the membership has fluctuated from time to time, the enthusiasm of its members has ensured that the society is one of the most popular on South Tyneside, and thought to be the oldest of its kind in the country. During the formation of the society, judging and viewing took place in the Robin Hood public house close by, due to the lack of facilities at Monkton. It wasn't for many years the Lord Nelson inn became host, and has remained so to the present time. The popularity of this autumn show is evident by the size of the marquee erected to house the exhibits. During the war years, the show was organised in a nearby school, it was thought the marquee would draw attention to the enemy, thus provoking an air raid. This photograph dates from the early 1940s.

22 Barefoot children playing in Grange Road without the danger of being knocked down by the motor car, in this view from 1905. The three buildings pictured are the Masonic Hall, Sunderland and South Shields Water Board offices, and the town hall respectively. The purpose-built Masonic Hall was officially opened in 1882, and is still used today for the purpose it was intended. The town hall was opened by the town's first mayor, Sir Charles Mark Palmer, and used as such until Jarrow was amalgamated with Hebburn, South Shields and Boldon to form the metropolitan borough of South Tyneside in 1974.

Grange Rd. Jarrow. 137.

23   The foundation stone of St. Bede's School was laid on 2nd February 1914. A dedication mass was offered at St. Bede's Church prior to a procession through the streets to the official opening ceremony three years later in 1917. This self contained modern building was actually two schools in one, the Harold Street entrance was used by the boys, and Howard Street for the girls, each school had separate facilities. The immaculately dressed staff of the boys' school are assembled here for the annual school photograph of 1939. Seated centre is headmaster Edmund Mc Peake, to his right are John Bradley and Mrs Mac Maughan, to his left are Miss Mc Menamy and Richard Little. Back row, left to right, are Miss Rafferty, Cuthbert Riddle and Miss Rogan.

24 The chancel at St. Paul's Church was founded in the year 681 before the arrival of Bede. The basilica wasn't built until later in the decade, and for many years were two separate structures until the erection of the tower in 685 – the same year the church was dedicated to St. Paul – when the chancel, basilica, and tower were recognised as one building. The present nave of the church was built over one thousand years later in 1866, at the same time the north aisle was constructed, completing the church as we know it today. It is believed the monks of the 8th and 9th centuries hid in the tower from the marauding Danes.

This photograph dates from 1912.

St. Paul's Church, Jarrow.

25 East Jarrow has always been synonymous with the Catherine Cookson novels, and quite rightly so, for this is the area where she was born and raised as Katie McMullen. Whilst distanced from the main body of the town, the east end was equally self sufficient, with a good assortment of shops, two chemical works and an ironworks, there was more than adequate employment for what was a modest population. Sadly, this part of town has disappeared, though a couple of streets did survive until the 1960s. East Jarrow was largely demolished during the 1940s making way for the Bede Industrial Estate. All that remains today are a few tattered photographs of the dusty streets, similar to this one of Swinburne Street in 1900, and a legacy of words courtesy of Katie McMullen.

26 As industry in Jarrow steadily grew, so did the need for a reliable transport service to shuttle the men to and from work, the electric tram-car was looked upon favourably. As the efficiency of systems in other towns was carefully monitored, the projected Jarrow system had to be both convenient and economically viable to operate smoothly. A vast network of tram lines snaked their way from the sheds at Tyne Dock – where the trams were garaged – through the streets to Western Road where the service was to terminate. Passengers wishing to travel beyond, could do so with the aid of horse drawn buses, which operated in conjunction with the tramcars. The first trial car of the Jarrow and District Electric Traction Co Ltd to make its debut, was car No 5, pictured here at the foot of Berkley St, on November 1st 1906. This crowd of youngsters – many barefoot – seem to be overcome with excitement at the prospects of a free ride. The system, which was powered by coal fired, steam driven generators, from a power station in Beech St, moved over in 1929 in favour of the motor bus.

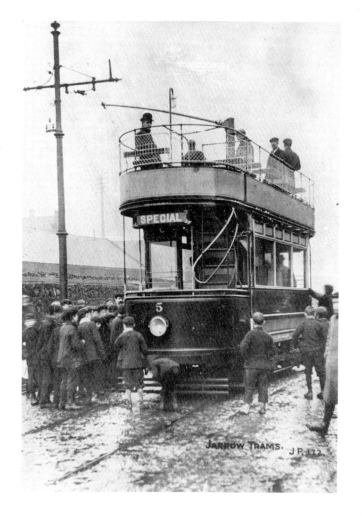

27   Butchers, bakers, and the proverbial candlestick maker, at some time or another in its chequered existence, Jarrow has had them all. Perhaps more butchers and bakers – 28 and 36 respectively – in 1920, just after the first war. In more recent times, quite a large proportion of meat eaten is imported from various parts of the world. Things were much different in 1905 when this photograph was taken, many butchers slaughtered on their premises, with others purchasing from slaughter houses throughout the region. The shop to the right of the accompanying photograph are the premises of butcher George Alexander in Western Road, where he offered parcels of meat and sausage, for 6d (2.5p) every Saturday evening prior to closing, and the advent of the refrigerator. Notice the tram lines, and the overhead cable bearers in position, awaiting the arrival of the first tram in 1906.

Western Road, Jarrow.

28 For many years Bede Burn Road has remained largely unchanged, the terraced houses look as good today as they did when they were first built. Some would argue, they look even better, having been subject to the northern weather for over a hundred years. The electoral roll from 1920, reveals this picturesque terrace was built most definitely for the middle class, with the community primarily consisting of upstanding and the well-to-do citizens of the town. Bank managers, school teachers, accountants, and architects among them, which could have had something to do with a by-law passed by the town council, preventing the sale of intoxicating liquor in this particular residential area. The handsome detached period houses should by no means be overlooked. Danesfield, prior to it becoming a maternity hospital, was a private residence, as was Fairholme, to the right of this picture from 1900. Fairholme, in more modern times, was utilised as a police hostel.

Bede Burn Road, Jarrow.

29   Another fine house in Bede Burn Road was Balgownie – built for consultant surgeon Dr. O'Neill – which incidentally was used for many years as a children's clinic after the closure of the children's health centre based at the town hall. Belsfield House, yet another charming residence, was converted at the beginning of the 20th century into St. Bede's convent and girls' school, and remained as such until 1958, when the students concluded their education at the newly-appointed St. Joseph's school at Hebburn. The continuation of 'nice houses' spilled over into what was to become York Avenue. Cornfields and pasture land were abundant in this part of town up until the 1920s, when houses first started to appear. It was deemed a desirable and fashionable place to live in 1928, when it was officially opened by H.R.H. Duchess of York. This photograph dates from 1953.

YORK AV. - JARROW

30 The lone cyclist is on what we know today as Butcher's Bridge Road, or the Lonnen as it is known locally. When this photograph was taken in 1949, the parish of St. Matthew had been established for 14 years. The central building in the centre of this picture – actually a glorified wooden hut – was the school hall which, when necessary, doubled as the church; the church as we know it today didn't make its appearance until about 1958. The building to the left is Belsfield House, a convent, and St. Bede's central school for girls. The school was divided into four houses, Milne, Newbolt, Barrie and Yeats. Whilst inter-school sporting activities were fun, the competition was fierce, with occupants of the four houses having equal enthusiasm, especially the netball team, who were presented with a silver league cup for the third successive year in July 1932, at Palmer's recreation grounds at Monkton. Sport was always encouraged at Belsfield, where cricket was very well played, but it was netball, and tennis, where the girls excelled during inter-house competition, perhaps encouraged by the presence of the members of the Jarrow Tennis Club.

31   The Tennis Club was established in the mid-1930s with a membership in excess of 50, but with the war years approaching, the enthusiasm was to wain causing the collapse of the club. In 1952, some of the original tennis club members and former pupils of Belsfield formed a group with the intentions of resurrecting it. The enthusiastic group busied themselves during the spring of 1952, preparing the run down courts for tournaments during the forthcoming summer. Much work was required to the old pavilion, which was in a state of collapse. Thanks to these energetic young people, Jarrow could once again boast a tennis club. The popularity was evident, with members having to queue for an hour or more, to get on court. Six wonderful years the members spent passing away the summer months before the land was required for a school extension in 1958. This photograph from 1954, of the St. Bede's Tennis Club members in the pavilion, is one of the only relics remaining from those long hot summer days at the Belsfield tennis courts.

32 Charles Mark Palmer's Shipbuilding and Iron Co was registered as a business in 1865, three years after his partner and brother George had retired from the company. Charles retained his position as chairman for a futher 28 years, until his own retirement in 1893. Palmer's was more than a shipyard, it rose to become an integrated industry and one of the first at that. Its operations at one point covered the bringing in of iron ore aboard its own fleet of vessels, from the company's own mines in Yorkshire. The population of Jarrow in 1851 at the inauguration of the Palmer Co was a mere 3,500, within ten years it had doubled to 7,000.

By 1871, the population had increased to a massive 18,000, and in 1891 it had accelerated to a staggering 33,000, a level at which it was to maintain for many years. With this influx of people, the town prospered beyond all expectations, vast amounts of money were made for both the company, and its work force.

33 In 1907 there was an almighty slump in shipbuilding, the whole of the industry was severely affected and Palmer's was no exception. By 1910, slow progress was being made, but the recovery was not going to happen overnight. The uncertainty of the future created a lot of anxiety, but the fractures were to be concealed by the outbreak of war. For Jarrow the war was to be the solution it was so desperately seeking, the anxiety seemed to disappear as if by magic. By 1918, Palmer's was working both against and around the clock, supplying the urgently required warships and merchant vessels. The town once again looked forward to a brighter future. It is many years since Palmer's gates finally closed, but with two million tons of shipping behind it, Jarrow is still a proud town and will enjoy a strong sense of achievement for a long time to come.

34 Very little was recorded of the town's development and industrial growth until the 17th century, however, a document held in Durham Cathedral states there was a coal mine in Jarrow producing coal as early as 1618. This is highly probable because of the proximity of Jarrow with the sea, and the easily recoverable coal beneath it. Mining in Jarrow didn't really get under way commercially until the beginning of the 19th century. Simon Temple came from a shipbuilding background and was reputed to have built the country's first two wooden frigates, to an extremely high standard. But it was coal mining he was to make, and lose his fortune (see introduction). This detailed drawing of Temple's notorious Alfred Pit dates from around 1810.

35   Although the motto remained, the original coat of arms of the Borough of Jarrow bears little resemblance to the one we were more familiar with. The first, in the accompanying photograph, dates from 1875, when the borough was established. The three crowns symbolise King Egfrid, who donated the land to Abbott Benedict, on which to build a monastery. The link with the Venerable Bede is depicted by the church, the fort is a symbol of a Roman station erected here by Agricola, one of the many fortifications he built from the mouth of the Tyne to the Solway Firth in A.D. 81. Jarrow's shipbuilding heritage is remembered with a three-masted vessel. In the later version of 1928, the dragon clutching the golden crescent was retained, as was the crown and the link with shipbuilding, though a different interpretation was employed. The church was replaced with an open book, perhaps a more appropriate way of remembering Bede. Finally the shape of the crest was simplified, and after being registered in London, the new insignia went on exhibition in the town.

36 Many of the town's public houses were tied to one brewery, with the exception of the free house, who could stock as many ales from different brewers as they thought fit. There were many small brewers in the region, Arrol, Nimmo, and Flowers, all of which have now disappeared. The most popular in Jarrow were the ales from Newcastle Breweries Ltd, who later became Scottish & Newcastle. Newcastle ales were in plentiful supply at the Staith House in Pearson Place. Publican John Rafferty, licensee from 1922 to 1930, is photographed in the doorway with two of his regulars in 1925. On the inside, in the men-only bar, pipe smoking men would congregate around an enormous black leaded, coke burning stove, each having a tale to tell. Ladies were admitted on the understanding they were to use the 'select' or the 'snug' – a tiny sitting room – partitioned from the main body of the bar. Officers, representing the Weights and Measures Authorities, were responsible for fair play, it wasn't unusual for publicans to attempt to give short measure. The notice displayed in the window of the Staith House states, a visit to these premises by the officers found everything in order.

37 By 1936, more and more people were being rehoused on new housing estates, leaving behind the filth and squalor they had lived in most of there lives – not by choice I hasten to add. People were no longer to speak ashamedly of rats and mice running across their faces as they slept, no longer would they have to suffer the multitudes of beetles they shared their homes with, and worry no more whether or not the fire grate was about to fall from the wall. The days of balancing precariously on the rickety wood worm ridden stairs which gave entrance to their homes were over. Perhaps the biggest nuisance of all was the bedbug. It became practice for the authorities to insist, that where tenants were displaced from clearance areas, or unfit habitation, had to suffer the indignity of having their furniture and effects fumigated prior to them taking over new property. The council's insistence was a complete success, resulting in the eradication of the demon bug. This photograph of Back George Street dates from 1915.

38   It is little wonder why Jarrow was referred to as 'Little Ireland', just glance at surnames of the 'lads' in the accompanying photograph, who were exponents in their own right in the game of football, good enough to play their way to St. Bede's first team. Football has always been popular in Jarrow, whether you were kicking the ball around the back lanes, or selected to play for one of the town's many teams, in a Sunday morning league, the enthusiasm remained the same. The line up for the revived St. Bede's football team season 1951-1952 reads, back row, left to right: Raymond O' Connor, Frank Sullivan, Tom Morrow, Jim Joyce, Gerard Blackburn and Bill Mc Guire. Front row, left to right: Joe Mc Keown, Joe Kelly, Hughie Smith, Frank Weir and John Cassidy.

39 By 1946, much had been achieved to improve the quality of life, the council wasted no time or effort to attract new industries to Jarrow. Together with the assistance of the North East Development Council and the Board of Trade, an oil installation terminal was developed in the east end of the town, with the capability of storing up to 4 million gallons of petroleum spirit and fuel oil in its enormous tanks. Daily deliveries of the precious luiqids were made by rail, on a specially constructed mineral line, terminating inside the terminal. During the late 1950s, a pumping station was erected on the riverside, enabling the fuel to arrive by both sea and rail. The ships pumped their cargo ashore to the nearby storage tanks via a network of pressurised pipes. Not only did this dual system remove pressure from the overworked rail link, but it was to create a marked increase in productivity within the terminal. Shell and British Petroleum were the two major companies attracted to this site, chiefly because of its convenient location and proximity to the North Sea. As the success of the terminal unfolded, further tanks mushroomed on the horizon on the north side of the river, as further developments got under way. This aerial photograph of the still developing complex was taken in 1958.

40 A visit in 1945 of Sir Stafford Cripps MP, president of the Board of Trade, was to inject new life into the town with the building of the Bede Industrial Estate, which attracted many new industries to Jarrow and generated a lot of very welcome business. The plethora of medium-sized factories manufactured everything, from resistors to footwear and raw materials for the chemical and textile industries, though much of the work was for women. Nevertheless, the employment opportunities the factories brought were a vital contribution to the towns on going recovery. More companies were attracted to Jarrow as the planning department at the town hall fitted the remaining parts of the jigsaw, to complete the image of what was rapidly becoming a modern go-ahead town, with an abundance of decent houses for those who were attracted to it. A new Jarrow was changing out of all recognition from the old. This photograph of the Bede Industrial Estate dates from 1948.

41   In the 18th and 19th centuries, the River Tyne was answering to the demands of industry for the import and export of produce. Chemical works, salt production and a variety of other industries were springing up on either side of the Tyne, seeking means of transport for their goods, and the conveying of raw materials to these industries. The Tyne had to be improved by dredging, and widening, to accommodate the unpredictable river traffic. Coal was being shipped to the south of the country from Jarrow staithes as early as 1803. The unladen vessels arriving daily to collect their cargo, carried only sand as ballast. Pit owner Simon Temple prepared an area to deposit this ballast, and for many years the sand hills were to grow into small mountains and were visible on Jarrow's horizon, until the 1950s. As the number of ships using this gold mine of a river increased, so did the demand for ship repairing with docking facilities. This photograph from 1922 shows one of Jarrow's lesser known industries, that of cement production.

42   Due to the success of the Palmer Empire, Gavin Smith and his consortium of businessmen recognised the need for a yard specializing in ship repairs close to the mouth of the Tyne. A price was negotiated for a site on the south bank, and work on a dry dock promptly commenced in 1885. Whilst many thousands of tons of earth were excavated, wooden buildings were erected; these were to become the fitting, joiner and boiler shops. A paint shop and material stores department were also created in another part of the yard. In 1889, offices were built, cranes erected, and a work force assembled.

The Mercantile Dry Dock and Engineering Co was in business, and was to repair hundreds of vessels from the four corners of the earth for nearly a century; as the order book swelled, so did the work force. By 1890, the need for a second dry dock became evident, as the queues of ships moored in the Tyne awaiting repair. Number two dock was opened on 4th August 1892, eventually dry dock number three came along in 1908, and number four in 1960. Pictured is the construction of a deep water quay in 1954.

43 The fifties and sixties saw a fairly stable and hopeful period with a sustained, if irregular, stream of colliers, tankers, and cargo boats coming alongside for refit and repair. Number four dock was completed to accommodate the larger vessels that were now beginning to make up the worlds fleet. Hopes were high, for these were the days of prosperity, the times of plenty. A chance for the 'Jarra Lads' to walk in the sunshine, not under the constant clouds of unemployment and poverty, reminiscent of the thirties. The company became a subsidiary of Northeast Coast Ship Repairers in 1966, and became a constituent company of Court Line in 1977, latterly operating as part of the giant British Shipbuilders Ltd. The Tyne Ship Repair Group were to take over the yard's operations until its demise in 1981. Pictured is the giant number four dock just after its completion in 1960.

44   Prior to the arrival of Sir John Jarvis and the Surrey Fund, a social centre for the unemployed had been organised in the disused Springwell Paper Mills by the churches in Westminster London, under the direction of Lloyd Greening. The aim of the Surrey Fund was to bring fresh hope to the people of Tyneside, to provide them with pleasant surroundings, and hopefully a brighter future. To teach them new skills and ultimately find them permanent work. The first objective was Jarrow, the worst hit town in the country with an unemployment level set at 80 percent. These figures meant that Jarrow had to move forward, and with the help of Sir John, was to do just that. The £40,000 he brought with him was used carefully towards easing the hardship of the good people of Jarrow. A Personal Service League in the south provided nearly 50,000 items of clothing, bedding, and the much needed children's clothes. This photograph was taken on 14th June 1933 at the opening ceremony: Mayor Councillor Dodds, centre, and to his right, The Very Reverend Preben Austin Thompson, Rural Dean of Westminster.

45 Jarrow was a crowded town in the thirties and the provision for open spaces was looked upon as a vital necessity. The creation of the 20 acre Monkton Dene Park, provided work for 1,000 long unemployed men, each being employed for one calendar month, with preference going to men with dependent families, but eventually everyone was to get his share. Most turned up, for work their feet, so poorly shod, prevented them from doing a satisfactory days work. Each man had the opportunity of obtaining a new pair of boots, a luxury these men had long since forgotten. Altogether 910 pairs of quality boots were donated, courtesy of the Surrey Fund. In addition to the creation of the park, the men assisted in the erection of two pavilions, one at the Jarrow cricket ground, the other at the Blackett Sports Club. From the very beginning, the success or the failure of the Surrey scheme depended upon the provision of permanent work, all of the on-going activities were engineered towards this ultimate goal.

This photograph is of the recently completed Monkton Dene Park

46 The Jarrow instruction centre was to prove its worth to the unemployed, who channelled their energies into something worthwhile. In 1933, a football league comprising of 24 teams was formed, the boots, strips, and accessories were supplied by the readers of The Times newspaper and Surrey sportsmen. Because of this further act of generosity, just a small amount of money was required from the Surrey Fund enabling it to be used for more worthwhile causes. This league proved most successful, it attracted huge crowds to every game. Two thousand spectators attended the final at the Campbell Park ground, at which Sir John 'kicked off', and presented the trophy. This photograph was taken at the final of the 1933-1934 season

47   The men of Jarrow were encouraged to return to physical fitness with the assistance of the council, who, during the winter months, granted permission for the public baths to be used as a gymnasium. No fewer than 4,000 attendances were recorded, extra sessions were organised most afternoons, to accommodate the fitness-hungry men. The council requested, during the summer months, the public baths be used for what they were intended, and the group was asked to continue their physical fitness at the Drill Hall, where training would continue both in and out of doors. A boxing section was well under way and, more recently, the formation of a rugby football club. These activities were under the watchful eye of Lt Commander Melville R.N. (retired) who was the executive committee's resident representative in Jarrow, sports organiser, and physical training instructor. This photograph of the men in action was taken in 1935.

48 The young people of Jarrow were not forgotten. The interest shown by His Royal Highness King George V and the interest he had in boys' clubs resulted in the introduction of his personal secretary, Commander Adams, to Sir John Jarvis. The outcome of which was a special grant, to begin a boys' club in Jarrow, through the Durham County Association of Boys' Clubs. The now disused police station in High Street, was thought the ideal venue for such a club, the nominal rent was attractive enough for the project to go ahead. The materials for decoration were provided – which was undertaken by the boys – with a grant of £500, which also assisted in the maintenance costs. This photograph of the boys on an educational trip to the old monastery ruins was taken in 1934.

49 Such grants were not available under the terms of the Surrey Fund, but in isolated cases such as these, a donation towards the welfare of the boys and girls of the town involved in something so worthwhile and well-organised, was accepted under the grounds of it being advantageous to the boys and girls during the difficult years of adolescence. The boys were encouraged to attend the annual camp, with 50 percent of the cost of such 5/- (25p) per head offset by the fund. Among the girls activities were dressmaking and a choral society. The young girls in the accompanying photograph from 1934 were actively involved in folk dancing and displayed their talents at concerts staged in the town.

50 The ancient spring of St. Bede, to give it its correct title, is more commonly known as Bedeswell. In the northern counties of England, many ancient wells and springs still exist, which from the remotest periods of English history possess a legendary and popular interest. This is identified in some cases with the Roman occupation which merged into the early development of another civilisation, and have sometimes been connected with a local or titled saint. Many of these wells have been associated with peculiar customs and ceremonies from a dark and distant past. As late as 1740 it was still the prevailing custom to bring children to St. Monkton who were troubled with disease, when a crooked pin was dropped into the well. It is recorded, as many as twenty children were brought together on a Sunday to experience the power of the 'magic water'. Dropping pins into these wells was more common in Cornwall, Ireland and Wales, but by no means limited to these areas, and it is from this practice they were to become widely known as 'pinwells'.

Venerable Bede Well, Jarrow.

51 It is thought, a bedeswell was a boundary marker, and this could well be true, when you take into consideration the location of this particular well. The Anglo Saxon translation of bedeswell is 'bedanwylla' and the ancient Romans termed it 'badeswelle', derived from the word Be'd (a prayer) and it is from here the word bead derives. Bedeswell loosely translated means 'the well of prayer'. There is a particular good example of a bedeswell at Ham, in the county of Wiltshire. In 1908 the parish council of Monkton was anxious to take steps towards the preservation of the well and to raise £200 for the sole purpose, believing the industrial and commercial encroachment of neighbouring Jarrow threatened to destroy this ancient watering place. These two very different photographs of the well date from 1895 and 1902 respectively.

52 Lambs snack foods was founded in 1937 at a small factory in Birtley, manufacturing potato crisps. Because of the demand for this popular snack, larger premises were sought, a site in Jarrow was purchased and by 1949 the building in Ferry Street was converted. The factory was installed with the most modern, and up-to-date machinery, so that in the cooking and packaging, the crisps are untouched by hand. The output rose to fifteen times that of the former factory in Birtley. A process was developed at the factory monitoring potato quality, making this one of the most efficient plants in the country. As the business went from strength to strength, the need for a warehouse became necessary, premises in Staple Road were utilised until the business was purchased by Tudor Foods Ltd in 1959, when the land was required by the council for the construction of the Market Square housing development. This photograph was taken in 1952.

53   Civic dignitaries, businessmen and members of the
Masonic movement, joined a
crowd of 5,000 townsfolk, to
march in procession through
the streets of Jarrow, terminating at Clayton Street for
the solemn ceremony of unveiling and dedicating a
monument to those who fell
in the Great War. Traditionally,
on the eleventh day, of the
eleventh month, on the eleventh hour, a two-minute silence is observed as a mark of
respect to those who gave
their lives for King and Country. As the years passed, the
elements ravaged the twenty-
foot tall sandstone monu-
ment, to a degree where the
inscription was illegible. Recently, restoration work was
carried out to restore it to its
former glory and rightful
prominent place in Jarrow's
history.

54   Mr. G. Mure Ritchie, chairman of Palmers – who donated the monument to Jarrow Corporation – performed the unveiling ceremony on 6th November 1921, witnessed by a guard of honour from the regiment of the Royal Engineers. The Reverend Williams, rector of Christ Church, offered prayers and after a two-minute silence, Reverend Ritson, rector of Jarrow, recited the blessing. Upon completion, the 'last post' was sounded by buglers from Palmer's band. The Mayor Mr. Andison took possession of the deeds, transferring the cenotaph to the custody of the Borough for safe keeping. The inscription on the monument reads: 'Erected by the directors and shareholders of Palmer's Shipbuilding and Iron Co Ltd, to record their appreciation of the patriotism of 1,543 from the Jarrow and Hebburn works in joining His Majesty's forces for service in the Great War 1914-19, and in grateful and honoured memory of those who made the great sacrifice for their country, and who's names are inscribed on this monument.' These rare photographs marking the occasion, show the procession in St. John's Terrace, and the Honourable Robert James laying a wreath on behalf of the directors of Palmer's, at the base of the monument, overlooked by the Reverend Ritson.

55 After the two world wars, practically every town and village in the country had a welcome home party for its heroes' and heroins' safe return. Many churches throughout the land offered services in thanksgiving and Jarrow was no exception, street parties and carnivals were in abundance to celebrate both victories. Jarrow's welcome home committee, like others, was finding it difficult to arrive at a decision as to what form the welcome home to returning men and women from the forces should take. At a meeting in the council chambers it was suggested a gift of a cigarette case may be appropriate for the men, whilst a compact would seem perfect for the women. This suggestion was deemed reasonable, and the motion carried. The homecomings were to be spread over quite a long time, so was the cost of the gifts. On each occasion the mayor had £500 and £1,000 respectively – most of which were donations - at his disposal, and was to be used at his discretion. This photograph dates from 1919.

56 Lamplighters were eventually to disappear from the landscape after the introduction of electricity, and this was to happen in Jarrow in the early 1900s. On 22nd February 1900, a special meeting was called at the Corporation offices to discuss the introduction of electric light, both in our streets and homes. It was moved, the County of Durham Distribution Co, was to be entrusted with the illumination of our neighbourhood. The price of the power offered was extremely favourable: at 7d (3p) per unit for the first one hundred hours per quarter, and 1d per unit for subsequent hours, these rates were to fight off all serious competition. Alas, it was only the main streets and thoroughfares which were to enjoy the benefits of electricity. Gaslight was to remain the prime source of street lighting, though automated up until as late as the early 1960s. This photograph taken in 1953, at the junction of commercial Road, and Buddle Street, typifies the duties of a small army of men employed solely to maintain the equipment.

57 Local dialect changes from region to region, a fact we are all well aware of. Perhaps the Geordie accent is more changeable than most. A few short miles up the coast into Northumberland, the jargon is completely different to that which is spoken south of the Tyne, which again, has many variations. Because of the harsh Geordie dialect, it is understandable how visitors to these parts associate the 'local twang' with the Welsh accent. Everyday pursuits are perhaps the best place to stumble over humorous and obscure little words which have found their way into our language. For example, a 'jumper' is not an item of clothing worn in the winter, it was in actual fact a conductor who stepped from one tram to another to assist in the collection of fares during busy periods. Wheeltappers were exactly what their name suggests, and offered their services to both the tram, and railway industries. Pictured is the official opening of Jarrow's light railway in November 1929. The line was constructed by John Lant and Co, and operated from Jarrow station and terminated close to the salt grass in the east end of the town.

58 Whilst we are on the subject of dialect, this could be an opportune moment to reflect on other occupations with strange sounding names. A 'lumper', I am reliably informed, is the correct name for a person who manoeuvres ships to their moorings on the waterways. 'Putters' belonged to the mining fraternity, they placed the empty tubs in position to be filled with coal, and the 'hadder ups' and the 'bumper ups' worked in close harmony with the riveters in the shipbuilding industry. My own particular favourite is the gentleman who regarded himself as a 'transparent wall maintenance officer', to you and me: a window cleaner. Sadly most of these occupations are no longer with us, but their names will live forever as part of our rich heritage. Riveters, 'hadder ups' and 'bumper ups' are pictured here at the Mercantile Dry Dock in 1942.

59   In past times, the Pyman Bell Co was associated with the timber industry. But when the company commenced trading in 1873, exporting coal was the main theme of their business, and remained this way until the turn of the century. From this time, until the mines were nationalised in 1947, the business turned towards the supply of mining timber to the coal industry from its depots in the north-east. The 1950s witnessed the concentration of these activities into fewer minefields as the industry became mechanised. It was about this time the company joined what was a growing industry in Jarrow, that of sawn wood. After the purchase of the Sunderland firm of J.W. Wilson, it was to supply the building industry with varying types and qualities of timber. During the 1960s, the company set up a department for the supply and erection of suspended ceilings. The Pyman Bell Co ceased trading in Jarrow during the early 1980s. Various other companies traded in wood in this area, one of them, Denny Mott and Dickson, has long since gone, but two others, Edmund Robson and Co and M. H. Southern, are both active in the industry. This photograph dates from the early 1950s, and shows the part of Jarrow given over to the timber trade.

60   Like many other towns wich have grown up rapidly, Jarrow had many needs. One in particular was need for a bridge spanning the passenger and mineral lines at Jarrow railway station, linking the north and south sides of the town. In 1884, a decision was taken to erect a stairway connecting the two points, which very quickly became known, not surprisingly, as the 'station stairs'. By 1891 plans were being made to elaborate upon this simple stairway, because of the danger it created during inclement weather. A glance at the accompanying illustration shows – almost without words – how this could be achieved. It was thought a bridge at this location would greatly reduce the distance between St. John's Terrace and Ellison Street, for horse-drawn vehicles and hand carts.

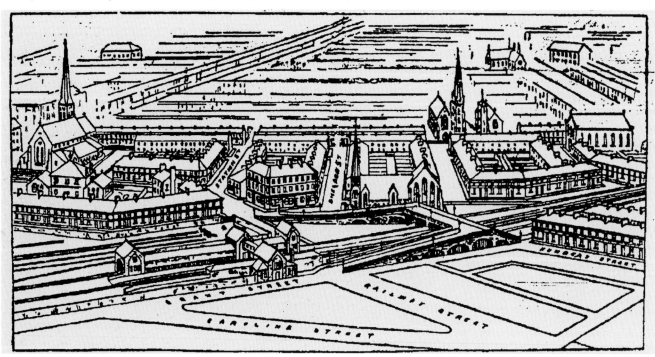

61   The proposed 30 ft wide bridge was to be constructed of concrete, reinforced with steel girders, and have a total length of 520 ft including the approaches. A gradient of 1 in 13, at the Clayton Street approach, and 1 in 12 at the other, was deemed somewhat steep, but not steep enough to create problems and cause an impediment to traffic. Alas, an acute shortage of money prevented any further progress of the structure. Alternatively the existing walkway was reinforced enough to support the weight of a glass-sided canopy, and was to remain this way until its demolition in the 1970s. This photograph taken from Wear Street dates from the 1950s.

62   Paper manufacture in Jarrow commenced in 1841 by Thomas Bell, until 1860, when the mill he operated was taken over by successful businessman and Quaker William Henry Richardson, who after employing scores of men, women, and children at the paper mill at Springwell, channelled his energies into worthwhile activities for the good of the town, particularly in the cause of education, eventually rising to the positions of chairman of the first school board in the country, and Justice of the Peace. Following a series of disastrous fires at the paper mill, a severe slump in the industry, and the accidental death of Richardson in 1923 at his home in Monkton Lodge, the ailing mill was sold and eventually dismantled, which inevitably added to the growing list of Jarrow's failing industries. During the troubled 1930s the disused mill became temporary home to an instruction centre. In the 1960s Smiths furnishing group used it as warehouse and offices, and in March 1998, after the evacuation of its final resident, a plant hire company, the property was demolished to make way for Mill Dene, a smart new housing complex.

WILLIAM HENRY RICHARDSON, J.P.,
Chairman of the first School Board.

63   In 1861, the Wesleyan's, constructed a day, and Sunday school in the market square, education at this time, was neither free or compulsory, and the nonconformists introduced the concept of Sunday schools. Each Sunday, children would receive, not only religious instruction, but also a basic grounding in reading, writing, and arithmetic. This allowed the children to earn an income during weekdays, to supplement the family income. By 1870 the introduction of an education act came into force allowing elected school boards to finance new schools, and provide financial assistance to religious schools, providing their standards of education were approved by education inspector's. Due to the lack of educational facilities, the act did not implement compulsory education up to the age of thirteen, but left it to the discretion of the local board of education. This photograph of class 3 at the Ellison Church of England school, was taken in 1950.

64 It was Jarrow's school board who introduced compulsory education up to the age of thirteen, after the construction of the country's first board school, this was the Grange Board School in the early 1870s. After the completion of Monkton government school in 1873, education still wasn't free, but government grants reduced the fees met by parents. In order to qualify for one of these coveted grants, evidence was to be made available to inspectors of an adequate standard of education. A strict regime was implemented to achieve – what seemed – impossible objectives. Jarrow Central School was the catchment area for Jarrow, Hebburn and Felling for pupils just failing to gain entry to grammar school in the eleven plus examination. This photograph, taken at the Christmas party at the Central School, with pupils from the third, fourth and fifth years, comes from 1951.

65 It is only in very recent times since the ancient game of bowls has been played indoors. This once summer pursuit was played in Greece, Egypt and Rome as early as the 8th century, and possibly before. It was during the 10th century, that the game became popular in Europe. Bowls has been played in Jarrow since 1876, and is still played today with the same enthusiasm. Perhaps television has assisted in many ways to keep the sport as popular as ever. In 1946, William Fyfe, a Scot by birth and resident of Jarrow, bowled himself into the record books with an amazing 360 games in one season. This record was deemed a challenge for many years to lovers of the game, but went unequalled, the closest being one hundred games away from the target. Bill – to his friends – was a member of three Jarrow clubs, and a founder member and backbone of the West End Club. This photograph of the bowling greens at West Park dates from 1921.

Bowling Greens, Jarrow Park

66 Because of the welcome increase in trade on the River Tyne, and with vessels of varying sizes arriving daily, some laden with cargo, others for repair, concerns were rising as for the safety of the workforce in the busy Tyne ports. In the 19th century, the Port of Tyne Sanitary Authority arrived at the conclusion a quarantine hospital, possibly isolated from the mainland, could be the solution to the problem. The idea of a floating hospital emerged, and by 1885, building work eagerly commenced. The successful launch of the hospital occurred on 2nd August 1886, and was to be moored at Jarrow. The hospital offered care for seamen from around the world, suffering from rare and infectious diseases contracted abroad. It was thought, the floating hospital would contain such diseases and reduce the risk of contamination with people either side of the river. It became the practice, and eventually an obligation, of vessels entering the Tyne, to fly the 'Yellow Jack', a flag which signified the ship was arriving from foreign parts.

67   A new addition to Jarrow's skyline was visible as from April 1948, an impressive monster crane was erected at the Mercantile Dry Dock. The installation of the monotower crane, rising 180 feet above the river front, is part of the extensive modernization being carried out by the firm. The sight of the crane on the horizon became a constant reminder of the unique Palmer cranes which domineered the skyline for so long. The crane is capable of lifting a remarkable 15 tons at a 90 ft radius, and 6 tons at a radius of 126 ft. It was designed to travel on rails, similar to that of a train, and served three dry docks. It was envisaged, this welcome addition to the company's modern facilities was to be an invaluable asset to speedy and efficient repairs. One of its first tasks was to assist in the repair of the 6,000 ton Norwegian vessel 'Ingeren' who suffered severe bottom damage by ice packs in the Elbe.

68 Because of the town's increasing population in the 1940s and '50s, and the evacuation of the inhabitants of the town centre to the newly appointed houses at Primrose and Hedworth, the need for schools, shops and places of worship became evident. The parish of St. Joseph, at Hedworth, was formed, and services were held in the nearby 'Boldon Lad' public house, prior to the church being built. The first church was a simple wooden structure erected close to the school, which served the parish until the mid-1970s, when the present church was built, and the late Fr. Cristopher Rice installed as parish priest. Saint Mary's Parish at Primrose was inaugurated in 1952. The church was consecrated and the inaugural mass was concelebrated by Bishop Mc Cormick of the diocese of Hexham and Newcastle, the newly appointed parish priest, Fr. Mc Donald and Fr. Avery on 2nd February 1952. Also present in the congregation were the Mayor Councillor Mothersdale, and the Mayoress Councillor Violet Hope.

69 The original Palmer Memorial Hospital was situated in Clayton Street, and was opened in 1871 by its founder Charles Mark Palmer. Intended for the sole use of his employees, it was maintained by an annual contribution from the company and subscriptions from the workforce. Because of the deplorable living conditions in Jarrow towards the latter part of the 19th century, poor sanitation, together with large numbers of people sharing inadequate housing, disease was inevitable, and sadly it was usually the children who suffered most. Because of this problem, a substantial part of the hospital was given over to their care and recovery. The hospital was dedicated to the memory of Palmer's first wife Jane, who passed away in 1865. She was dedicated to charitable events and concerns, and to the welfare of the people of Jarrow throughout her married life.

70 A magnificent stained glass window was erected inside the main entrance to the hospital, depicting biblical scenes of charity involving women. This was funded once again by the workforce, who revered Jane so dearly, and admired her care and generosity. During the 70s, the one hundred year old building was demolished, to make way for a modern hospital complex, built on the same site occupied by the original, and dedicated to its founder. The window, was carefully removed, refurbished, and replaced within the confines of the new building, and stands as a lasting tribute to an individual who did so much for the good of the town. The hospital was officially opened by H.R.H. The Princess Anne in June 1987. Photo, stained glass window Palmer Memorial Hospital.

71   In the Saxon word Gyrwy, long since corrupted into Jarrow, translated the word means marsh or fen and it was from this, Jarrow was to take its name. The 'slake' which it has been referred to for centuries is nothing more than a corruption of the word 'Jarrow's Lake'. On two occasions the 'slake' was used by the Romans to anchor their vessels at the mouth of the River Don, and by King Egfrid to shelter the whole of his fleet from the savage northern winter, and later the longboats of the plundering Danes. The 'slake' itself was an extensive waste, estimated to occupy a space of 1,000 acres, covered with water by the spring tides. Quite close the 'slake' were a scattering of country houses; the first was Jarrow Hall on church bank, another, Jarrow Lodge, was that of antiquarian and devoted enthusiast of ornithology John Straker, on the southern edge of the 'slake', where he housed a museum containing at least one of each species of migratory and native birds which frequented the area. Perhaps the most imposing of all was Simonside Hall, the home of magistrate Henry Major, which commanded splendid views of the River Tyne and neighbouring countryside. In more recent times, this sheltered basin was used for maturing timbers; the accompanying map dates from 1830.

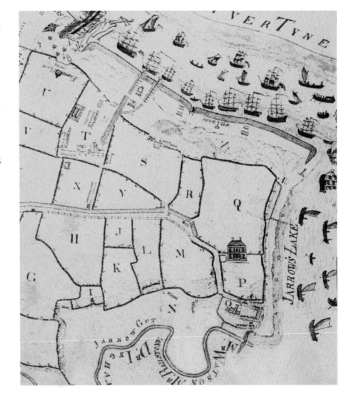

72 The manufacture of chemicals in Jarrow commenced around 1845. The first factory was the Jarrow Hill Co, commonly known as Jeffersons. These works were situated on land south of High Street, close to Quay Corner, and easily identified by the tall chimneys. Two further chemical works followed the success of Jeffersons, on rather a large scale that of Kenmires and Richardsons, close to Curlew Road. The industry flourished in town for many years, but were eventually forced out of business by major foreign competition. A recession in the chemical industry in Jarrow followed during the 1920s and '30s, but was to resurrect at the arrival of American giants Rohm and Haas, who first started trading in England from an office in London, under the name of Charles Lenig and Co. In 1954 a site was sought by Rohm and Haas, to manufacture some of the company's products. Because of the accessibility to rail, sea and air links, Jarrow was once again considered to be the perfect location. Initially a wide range of raw materials were manufactured for the leather industry. This photograph of the old jetty close to Quay Corner dates from 1945.

73 By the 1960s the company was trading under the name of Lenig Chemicals Ltd, and had increased their output with a new range of speciality resins for the paint, textile and paper industries. Extensions to the works were not only to secure jobs, but to increase their range of products and workforce with a plant solely for the manufacture of Oroglas acrylic sheet, and another for moulding powders, enabling the company to work at full power with a compliment of 500. This photograph, taken from Ellen Court, shows clearly the expanse of land taken over by Rohm and Haas. Prior to this the land lay derelict for many years after the demise of the Palmer Co.

74 Jarrow has the natural advantage of being situated close to the deep water of the River Tyne, and has always been connected by good roads, and rail communications to all centres of commerce. For many years, the townsfolk looked towards Palmer's for their bread and butter, but sadly Palmers is gone – never to return – and the vast area it once covered lay derelict, looming large and live, like a ghost from times gone by, waiting as if to haunt the present. Shipbuilding was not permitted here for forty years, under a clause in the contract of sale of the Shipbuilding Securities Co Ltd, who owned the land in the late 1930s. Nevertheless it was to this barren land the mighty John Jarvis was to look for any signs of renewed activity. 'If we can't build them, let's break them', he said, and with these words a new industry was conceived.

75 Though still in embryonic stages, ship breaking commenced with the purchase of a Greek vessel by the Surrey Fund which was sold to a firm of breakers on most attractive terms, to encourage them to test the viability of profitable work on our waters. The loss to the fund on this particular occasion was close to £1,000, a loss it could ill afford, but once again the northern territories rallied, and made good the losses; apart from this set back, the experiment was thought successful. Successful enough for Sir John to purchase – at his own expense – the 40,000 ton R.M.S. Olympic for £10,000. This was the second ship purchased by the scheme, and sold to the breakers for a handsome profit. The only cash to come from the now dwindling fund, was the shared expense of dredging the dock side. For a paltry £1000, eighteen months work had been provided for two hundred men on the Olympic alone. Many more craft including the 'Berengaria' were broken up in Jarrow. This picture of the 'Monarch of Bermuda' leaving the Tyne for Rosyth for completion of its demolition, dates from 1947.

76 Public houses around the east end of the town were few and far between owing to the precious land being used for industry and housing. In the early part of the century, prior to the invasion of the timber merchants to the area, chemical works were predominant. There was one other important industry – though nothing to do with chemicals – it was the Beehive iron works who manufactured iron rod, which was reputed to make the finest rivets on the river. The mastermind behind this ingenious little industry was John Elliott, who owned Beehive and supplied the majority of the yards both sides of the Tyne until its closure in the 1930s. The two surviving public houses in this region are the Allison Arms and the Alkali Hotel, the latter depicted here in this photograph from 1931, showing the landlord and some of his regulars preparing for a day trip.